FROZEN

BY BRYONY LAVERY

★

★

DRAMATISTS
PLAY SERVICE
INC.

FROZEN
Copyright © 2004, Bryony Lavery

All Rights Reserved

CAUTION: Professionals and amateurs are hereby warned that performance of FROZEN is subject to payment of a royalty. It is fully protected under the copyright laws of the United States of America, and of all countries covered by the International Copyright Union (including the Dominion of Canada and the rest of the British Commonwealth), and of all countries covered by the Pan-American Copyright Convention, the Universal Copyright Convention, the Berne Convention, and of all countries with which the United States has reciprocal copyright relations. All rights, including without limitation professional/amateur stage rights, motion picture, recitation, lecturing, public reading, radio broadcasting, television, video or sound recording, all other forms of mechanical, electronic and digital reproduction, transmission and distribution, such as CD, DVD, the Internet, private and file-sharing networks, information storage and retrieval systems, photocopying, and the rights of translation into foreign languages are strictly reserved. Particular emphasis is placed upon the matter of readings, permission for which must be secured from the Author's agent in writing.

The English language stock and amateur stage performance rights in the United States, its territories, possessions and Canada for FROZEN are controlled exclusively by DRAMATISTS PLAY SERVICE, INC., 440 Park Avenue South, New York, NY 10016. No professional or nonprofessional performance of the Play may be given without obtaining in advance the written permission of DRAMATISTS PLAY SERVICE, INC., and paying the requisite fee.

Inquiries concerning all other rights in the United States should be addressed to William Morris Endeavor Entertainment, LLC, 1325 Avenue of the Americas, 15th Floor, New York, NY 10019. Attn: Val Day.

Inquiries concerning all United Kingdom and foreign rights should be addressed to United Agents, 12-26 Lexington Street, London, W1F 0LE, England or info@unitedagents.co.uk. Attn: St John Donald.

SPECIAL NOTE

Anyone receiving permission to produce FROZEN is required to give credit to the Author as sole and exclusive Author of the Play on the title page of all programs distributed in connection with performances of the Play and in all instances in which the title of the Play appears for purposes of advertising, publicizing or otherwise exploiting the Play and/or a production thereof. The name of the Author must appear on a separate line, in which no other name appears, immediately beneath the title and in size of type equal to 50% of the size of the largest, most prominent letter used for the title of the Play. No person, firm or entity may receive credit larger or more prominent than that accorded the Author. The following acknowledgments must appear on the title page in all programs distributed in connection with performances of the Play:

FROZEN was first performed by
the Birmingham Repertory Theatre on May 1, 1998.

It was revised and revived at the
National's Cottesloe Theatre on July 3, 2002.

It received its New York Premiere at the MCC Theater on February 25, 2004.
Artistic Directors: Robert LuPone & Bernard Telsey
Associate Artistic Director: William Cantler

This production of FROZEN transferred to Broadway
at the Circle in the Square Theatre on May 4, 2004.
Roy Gabay, MCC Theatre, Harold Newman, Zollo/Paleologos & Jeffrey Sine,
Lorie Cowen Levy & Beth Smith, Peggy Hill, Thompson H. Rogers,
Swinsky/Filerman/Hendel, Sirkin/Mills/Baldassare & Darren Bagert

The author wishes to acknowledge the inspiration of Dorothy Otnow Lewis, M.D., and her work with Dr. Jonathan Pincus, concerning the neuropsychiatric characteristics of murderers as profiled in Malcom Galdwell's article "Damaged" (*The New Yorker*, February 24, 1997). Anyone wishing to read further about it should see Dr. Lewis's book *Guilty by Reason of Insanity* (Ballantine, 1998).

The author wishes to express her gratitude to Marian Partington, for her words and her courage. See *Salvaging the Sacred: Lucy, My Sister* by Marian Partington, first published in "The Guardian Weekend," May 18, 1996, subsequently "The Guardian Year 96," Fourth Estate Ltd, ISBN 978-1-85702-551-4, and now published by Quaker Books 2004, ISBN 978-0-85245-353-7.

Anyone wishing to learn more about the psychology
explored in this play should go to www.gladwell.com.

FROZEN won the 1998 Barclays Award for Best New Play in its original production at Birmingham Repertory Theatre in Birmingham, England, and later received its critically acclaimed London premiere at the Royal National Theatre in London, England, opening on July 3, 2002. It was directed by Bill Alexander; the set design was by Ruari Murchison; the lighting design was by Paul Pyant; and the original music was by Jonathan Goldstein. The cast was as follows:

AGNETHA .... Anita Dobson
RALPH .... Tom Georgeson
NANCY .... Josie Lawrence

FROZEN was given its U.S. premiere by MCC Theater (Robert LuPone, Bernard Telsey, Artistic Directors; William Cantler, Associate Artistic Director; John G. Schultz, Executive Director) at the East 13th Street Theater in New York City, opening on February 25, 2004. The production subsequently transferred to the Circle in the Square Theatre on Broadway, opening on May 4, 2004. It was directed by Doug Hughes; the set design was by Hugh Landwehr; the lighting design was by Clifton Taylor; the costume design was by Catherine Zuber; and the original music and sound design were by David Van Tieghem. The cast was as follows:

AGNETHA .... Laila Robins
RALPH .... Brian F. O'Byrne
NANCY .... Swoosie Kurtz
GUARD .... Sam Kitchin

FROZEN officially opened on Broadway at Circle in the Square Theatre on May 4, 2004, with the same cast and creative team as above and produced by MCC Theater (Robert LuPone, Bernard Telsey, Artistic Directors; William Cantler, Associate Artistic Director; John G. Schultz, Executive Director), Harold Newman, Zollo/Paleologos & Jeffrey Sine, Roy Gabay, Lorie Cowen Levy & Beth Smith, Peggy Hill, Thompson H. Rogers, Swinsky/Filerman/Hendel, Sirking/Mills/Baldassare, Darren Bagert. The fight direction was by Rick Sordelet; the makeup and tattoo design were by Angelina Avallone; the production management was by B.D. White; the dialect coach was Stephen Gabis; the production stage manager was James Fitzsimmons; the general manager was Roy Gabay; and the associate producers were Edmund & Mary Fusco.

The revised version of the text is the one published here to coincide with the MCC Theater production of the play.

CHARACTERS

AGNETHA

RALPH

NANCY

GUARD

PLACE

England.

TIME

The present.

FROZEN

ONE — FAREWELL TO NEW YORK

New York street sounds … busy, whirling traffic and voices. Stops abruptly as light reveals … Agnetha, hallway of her apartment, New York. Checking her airline tickets, passport.

AGNETHA. Yes.
yes.
yes.
yup.
yeah.
yo.
(All is ready. She looks around. Looks through a doorway.)
Bye room.
(Gives the room a little wave.)
Bye bedroom.
bathroom.
office.
(She salaams gravely.)
Bye home.
(They all get waves, thumbs up, high sings as appropriate. Until … she's ready. She picks up airline tickets, carry-on bag. She's ready. Then, she unclenches her jaw … and her teeth start chattering.)
Oh no.
I do not need this.
Not now.
Please.
(But it is now. She puts down her tickets. Her teeth chatter uncontrollably. She succumbs loudly to the chattering …)
er g-g-g-g-g-g-g
oo g-g-g-g-g-g-g

okay
out
good.
(She waits again. Then tears fill her eyes and she starts blubbing. She encourages herself to cry ... then bawl ... there is something deliberate and good-humoured about it ... as if she is two people ... one expressing emotion, the other encouraging it out ...)
mmmmuuuuuuurrr ...
mmmmmmaaaaaaaaaaa ...
yes, come on ...
wwwwwaaaaaaahhhhhhh ...
mmmmmmaaaaaaaaaahhh ...
come on ...
plane to catch...!
oh boy ...
(The bawling moves into keening and howling, so Agnetha must pick up her carry-on bag, which she screams into, muffling the sound somewhat. She screams and screams. Finally ...)
okay.
finished?
Finito?
(She checks.)
yes.
yep.
okay.
good.
(Picks up her travel documents, bag, etc. again.)
yes yes yes yup yeah yo
(She calls loudly through the walls.)
Sorry, Mrs. Lipke!
The Big Noise is leaving!
Sorry Mr. Chen!
Crazy Horse is outta here!
(She leaves for the airport. The sound of a large plane flying over ... heading towards ...)

TWO — FAMILY LIFE

The gentle chirrup, hum, buzz of an English garden …
Nancy, home, her back garden, evening, idly nipping buds off.

NANCY.　　　I should have gone round myself with those garden
　　　　　　　　shears.
　　　　　　　Mother and I've never seen eye to eye on shrubbery.
　　　　　　　I'm prune-to-a-dormant bud
　　　　　　　but she'll be instigating a slash-and-burn-regime.
　　　　　　　She's let her Clematis Montana Alba do its own thing.
　　　　　　　I said "they like their feet in the shade and their
　　　　　　　　head in the sun" but she's plonked it
　　　　　　　in a south-facing bed
　　　　　　　sandy soil
　　　　　　　and it's gone on the rampage over into next door's
　　　　　　　　specialty alpines.
　　　　　　　I offered to go round myself tomorrow and cut it
　　　　　　　　back for her
　　　　　　　but she says "It's Bridgnorth tomorrow"
　　　　　　　Always leaves it to the last minute and then its got to
　　　　　　　　be
　　　　　　　done This Minute Now Immediately.
　　　　　　　So I asked for volunteers but that was like getting
　　　　　　　someone to sign up for active service …
　　　　　　　Bob's got Nautilus training …
　　　　　　　and what's *that* all about…?
(A plane flies overhead. Nancy "tuts" gently.)
　　　　　　　been very happy with his flab till now
　　　　　　　and I always say "I'm very partial to your love handles"
　　　　　　　when we have a cuddle
　　　　　　　but
　　　　　　　well
　　　　　　　so I need one of the girls to look lively
　　　　　　　But Ingrid's "Off" Grandma at the moment because of
　　　　　　　The Make-Up Question
　　　　　　　so I think easier all round if I send Rhona …

9

but Rhona's so good I always put on her
and I try to be fair
so I gird my loins to tackle Ingrid
in spite of it being like negotiating with Attila The
  Hun these days ...
I've taken a Deep Breath ...
when suddenly crash Bang Wallop
Holy War breaks out upstairs! ...
"What Is It Now?" ... I go — and that's when Bob
  slithers out ...
he's so ... *sneaky* these days ...
no "Goodbye then Nancy love ... "
well
In The War Zone ...
There's a Max Factor Thick-Lash mascara wand
gone missing from Attila's *private* drawer
and who's Suspect Number One...?
Ingrid goes into Rhona's room
to obligingly fetch her for me,
drags her back by her *hair,* so I *separate* them
and look at Rhona.

(She smiles.)

She looks like a Panda!
Great black-rimmed eyes.
I say to Ingrid "go on, give her a bamboo shoot"
wrong thing to say ...
"Mum! Rhona's not *funny!*
You should take this *seriously*"
I say "Who takes *me* seriously about a ceasefire on
this Fighting?"
and I pop in "So ... Ingrid ... why don't you go
  round to
Grandma's for a bit of peace?"
and she's almost hooked when I add ... "And you
  could take
the garden shears while you're at it ... "
and she's off again "I'm just an unpaid scivvy in this
establishment ... I wish I was an orphan ... I wish
  somebody
would adopt me ... nobody loves me ...
everybody loves Rhona best ... "

I say hopefully "Now stop that nonsense …
I love you both equally in different ways"
I don't.
I don't love either of them *at all* at the moment!
Or Bob!
Or Mother!
Any of them!
They can all go to hell for all I care
(Quite close by, a van accelerates …)
but anyway
somehow it happens
Ingrid has me agreeing to let her go out
and chain of command's put the youngest soldier on
    secateur duty!
Little Panda.
My mother's going to think I'm letting *her* wear
makeup too young and be Reading The Riot Act! …
That's why Rhona's not back yet.
Yes!!!

THREE — A BAD PATCH

Ralph, in his room, washing his hands at a sink.

RALPH.   You know
it's one of those days
you're just going to do it
you might do it
I suppose mostly I'm a bit of a cold fish
(He dries his hands carefully on a small, clean towel.)
but then, these times
things hot up
It's been a bit of a bad patch for me …
fucking landlady …
pardon my French …
despite I told her I don't eat lamb
despite I told her I'm not a big eater …

11

despite I made that clear ...
turns up on the plate
and I've eaten it before I've said
"this isn't lamb is it...?"
and it *was* ...

(Takes a small bottle of hand lotion, pours a dollop on one palm, starts to rub it into both hands.)

and I've gone out with
hoojit ... Raymond Quantock ...
and that wassname from work ... Dick Bottle ...
and I've kept up with them putting it away ...
otherwise ...
and drunk five lagers
and two ...

(Counts in his head.)

... four ...
Jack Daniels
and I've gone over on that damn foot again ...
lightning strike of pain ...
and it's put me in a strop
nobody better mess me with
nobody better
been like ... offish
and ...

(He's on a street somewhere.)

I just see her
and decide
I'm going to get her in the van
I just want to keep her for a bit
Spend some time with her.
I just do it.
It's a rush of blood.
Hello.
Hello.
I said "Hello"
are you deaf?
It's rude to ignore people.
are you loony?
you're loony.
I'm only being polite.
No need to get the hump.

Not with me.
I just said "Hello."
Hello.
Hello.
Hello.
I'm saying "hello" to you.
Least you can do is make conversation.
Kind of world is this
folk can't be sociable?
Polite.
Least you can do is make a response.
It's Bad Manners if you don't.
Bad manners.
Rude.
I said "Hello"
Hello
Hello
Hello
Hello
Hello then ...
finally ...
finally ...
she goes
"Hello"

I think she quite liked me

oh yes
She was interested

the van's down here
it's only fifty yards away
it's convenient
obviously
the back door's not locked
because I've thought ahead
obviously
she wants to come

I've got cushions in the back
And a sleeping bag.

Obviously.

sometimes you're fucked by
circumstances
things don't go your way
(Picks something up. Regards it.)
the garden shears
I don't bargain for
but
in the event
they turn out
useful
and add to it all
passing off
efficiently
but
logistically
she's persuaded it's time
to get in the van
you make it work
she's in the van.

Lovely evening
Sunny ... but with a light southerly breeze ...

FOUR — NATURE TABLE

Nancy, Rhona's bedroom, seven months later ... a window overlooking the garden.

NANCY.   This is Leo.
(A small, threadbare soft-toy lion. She smiles slightly.)
He's bald where she played Hairdressers on him.
"Rhona's Rough Cuts"

Ingrid's making me a cup of coffee.
She's like the Catering Corps these past few days.

Mum, do you want a cup of hot chocolate?
Mum, shall we have a milky drink?
Mum, Cherry Bakewell?

I've lost nearly two stone.
I've gone back to smoking.
Cast Iron Excuse.
Even my Mother has to let me.

It's bad today because it's Rhona's
birthday tomorrow and they say
Missing Children often phone on their
birthdays
Get in touch ...
(She holds her stomach. Swallows.)
so I thought
clean her room
her Nature Table's a bit dusty

give me something to do

when she comes back
everything will be nice
everything be the same
everything familiar

that's gorse
with some sheep's wool tangled in it
From Brecon Beacons.
I got stuck between a lamb and its mother
the mother *ran* at me ...
I ran like billy-o
the girls fell over laughing!
Rhona found this in the gap ...
we had cheese and chutney sandwiches.
(A cold wind blows ...)
Brecon Beacons.
She loved that day!
Wales! She's maybe ...
(Thinks.)
No. We leafletted Wales.

this is her witch stone
it's a witch stone if it has a
natural hole in it.
See.
(Looks through it.)
you can see things in a witchy way …
it's magic.
(Holds it tightly in her hand, eyes tight closed. Making a wish.)
kept it there.

mmm.
(Puts it back exactly.)
What are you doing on here, Leo?

You live on the bed!

Somebody's been in here …
maybe Bob …
to primp and preen in private!
I know what's going on and
I know who with
It's all gone a bit softly-softly and undercover
what with The Disappearance …
but if it's over I'm Raquel Welch!

I   don't   care   !

These books are different.

Ingrid!
(It is stifling her …)
Washing up
Cleaning
Doing
Helping!
well it's not!
I don't want anyone in here moving her things
round I want to keep it exactly as it was!
If I have to get Bob to put a lock on that door
I will!

Rhona

where are you?

I know you're somewhere!

FIVE — MOVING ON

Ralph brings a suitcase into his room.

RALPH.   That incident up Scotland
          not down to me
          I operate in a southwards direction
          Midlands Leicester Home Counties

          Not fucking Scotland
          Not cold icy windy Scotland!
          Anybody with a *brain* would know that's Too Far!
          Too far from my centre of operations
          I mean you're looking at transportation
          something what over two hundred miles …
          where's the sense in that?
          Where's the efficiency?
          You've got to keep things *clean* in every sense
          I never touch *anything* outside an eighty mile radius
          of my centre of operations
          oh no
          oh no
          once you've got a site sorted
          well, you don't mess with *that*, do you?
          obviously
          but
          mud sticks

          I got 750 pounds for the van.
          Him who bought it

didn't notice the chassis's all rust
fuck him if he can't make a thorough check!

I'll get something a later reg.
That's been a bit of an unlucky vehicle for me.
So's this place.
Landlady …
despite when The police come here
they found nothing
despite it's clean
despite I'm clear
despite that …
has gone "sling your hook
don't want you here
go
clear off … "
and I've no comeback on it in law !
cunt
Fucking Cheek! … 'scuse me!
Kept it like a New Pin!

Who do they think they are?

Should be a law
You should have a guarantee of security
for your money

Good job I done planning here.
Good job I thought logistically …
had these in lock-up.

(Taps head.)

You've got to wake up very early to get ahead of me!
Oh yes
Oh yes!

(Videos are packed, titles mostly upright. He turns one round. Takes out a notebook. Refers to it.)

Lollitots
Lesbian Lolita
Little Red Riding Hood

(Beautiful, romantic, yearning music … sounds of summer countryside.)

Little Ones In Love

18

Child Love
Lesbian Lolita at School
(He turns a video the right way round … mock exasperation … he loves these videos.)

Lolita's Examination
Lolita's Auntie
Pre-Teen Trio

Sweet Patti
Sweet Susan
Little Linda
Baby Bonnie …

these cost!
What!!!
so I put them in safe storage
obviously.
Protect my investment.
I've had to get these from abroad!
Amsterdam, some of these!
France.
Denmark.

nobody's having these

they're precious
oh yes
oh yes

I'm going to have to safe-keep these in
my centre of operations
until I get a new residence
I'm going to have to get some sort of
protective filing system
I'm not sure that shed's efficient
dampwise …
(He makes a short list.)
now I'm moving on

new start

oh yes
oh yes
(A car drives off. Overhead steady thrum of plane as …)

SIX — THIS FLIGHT TONIGHT

Agnetha, on an aeroplane, laptop on her lap, keying sporadically … also drinking from a plastic cup …

AGNETHA.
(Keys.)
   "Serial Killing … a forgivable act?"
(She drains her drink. Presses the "Flight Attendant" summoning light … no response … Keys.)
   "Judicial Revenge … a political choice?"
(Pours non-existent drops of liquid from two or three small in-flight bottles of brandy into the glass. Presses Flight Attendant Call again … no response. Keys.)
   Brandy Refill … a Forlorn Hope?
   Yes … I think so … Close File … Save? …
   shit … E Mail … oh yes please …
(She starts writing furiously …)
   Dear David,
   Dearest Damn Fuck You Then David
   I hate you
   I hate hate hate hate hate you
   All the people on this flight are in mortal danger and
   it is your fault.
   You will be responsible for these multiple deaths
   as we plummet out of the sky
   into the sea a very very very long way down there
   right under where I am sitting.
   on *big* air
   over *big* sea
   it is your fault
   you and your Big News
   you and your Hilarious Damn Bad Behaviour have

alchemised me into
Miss Fudge Feeling of Washington Square
who is shit-scared of flying!
Give me back my real brain!
Hand over my native intelligence!
when we crash
because of you
because of you taking away my faith in anything at
   all …
I take innocent people with me …
Lily-White Souls perish here …

(She pours a non-existent drop of brandy into her glass.)
although the stewardess serving me deserves to die …
a lonely, painful, lingering, agonising death
for the impressive number of
times she has wilfully ignored my request for brandy
and for a certain radiant spitefulness over her
inability to provide me with a vegetarian meal …
I imagine pouncing,
sinking my teeth into her neck just above her
white pretty blouse and biting out her throat
murmuring all the time
"How's *this* for going with
The Meat Option?"

*(She covers her laptop screen with a "don't copy my homework" arm,
against her next-door neighbour. Looks out of the window.)*
Still over sea.

Watery death for us all then …
Lovely, violent in-flight movie
Many good and worthless men perished
in explosions of bright red blood.

I thought of you.
(Her eyes fill. She wipes them surreptitiously … then.)
you bastard
you make me frightened of everything!
(The plane flies on. Ping of "Fasten seat belts" sign flashing on …)
Oh   my   God   !
(Reads computer.)
SEND?

Why not?
(The plane flies on.)

SEVEN — FLAME

Nancy, smart suit, drink, her house, four years later.

NANCY.   It always works …
           but it was magnificent tonight!
           I get whoever's in charge of introducing
           to say quite simply …
           "from the organisation *FLAME* … "
           Mrs. Nancy Shirley …
           and I find if you just give it a minute
              … they settle …
           and then I go …
(She is in a school hall, many silent people.)
           Ladies and gentlemen of the …
           and I fill in where we are …
           tonight it was a Parent/Teachers thing
           in Spalding …
           Ladies and gentlemen of the *whatever* …
           on April 17th, 1980,
           my daughter,
           Rhona …

           and I pick up her photograph …
           walked out of my house
           to go to her Grandma's house
           she never got there
           she never came back
           she was ten.
           She's been missing for
           five years.
           She will be fifteen years old tonight.
           I know she's alive.
           I have Faith.

22

Every night I pray
that whatever reason is stopping her coming home
will be removed
and that she'll phone
or write
or just knock on the door
and say "Mum, it's me"

Bob says he always watches that bit
it gives him a chill down his back he says
I've got him giving me lifts to these dos
it's brought us closer together,
cemented us
stopped that nonsense
with that Nautilus trainer woman
I've got him on jogging ...
he said "when you showed our Rhona's
photograph tonight, I thought, we're going
to get lucky this time ... "

and then I pick up the *other* photograph
and go ...

This ...
is Robert Greaves.
He disappeared on his way to
Boy Scouts on September 14th 1976.
He was fourteen.
Today's his birthday ...

you could have heard a *pin* drop ...

He's twenty-three ...
And four weeks ago he walked through
his parents' front door in Braintree, Essex,
and said "Mum, I'm back"
because we at *FLAME* found him!
Even though my little girl
my Rhona is still out there
I *rejoice* for Mr. and Mrs. Greaves
that our organisation

was able to reunite them
with their Robert ...

and Bob has the leaflets ready ...
because *FLAME* is about
just that ...
keeping that flame of hope alive
keeping it burning
so that our missing children
can see its light
and feel its warmth
and come towards it!

it's funny
I feel I was born to do this
I found nothing so easy to do as this
it's funny
but this is when I feel most alive ...

(Returns to her room.)
so ...
I'm not best pleased to get back to a
drunk Ingrid
ash tray piled
another fag burn on the settee arm ...
she says
"I had a bad dream
I'm in the frozen frozen Arctic
I've lost somebody
the body's under the ice
but it's getting harder and colder
the ice is building up ... "
I say "no wonder, you've let the thermostat
go off ... "
but she *wails* like a great soft thing ...
says ...

"I look for a hole
I look for a seal hole
but there's no hole
the body's down there
but it's all getting whiter"

(Pause.)

> I say well never mind do you want some
> drinking chocolate
> but she's off again
> "but do you know what I do then?"
>
> and I say no what
> and she laughs
>
> daft mad laugh
> and says
> "Oh
> I go inside of course
> to get warm"

(Pause.)

> Bloody girl!
>
> Bloody girl!

(A confused explosion of time markers … New Year bells … bonfire fireworks … Christmas … time passing … clocks.)

EIGHT — TATTOO YOU

Ralph, summer shirt, bench. He has tears in his eyes. Twenty years later.

RALPH.   Oya
            Oya
            Oya
(Limping … sits down, rubbing his ankle.)
> Fuck … this fucking hurts!
> Stinging!
> Oya!
> But you got to suffer for something worthwhile!
>
> Oh yes
> Oh yes

25

(Pulls up his trouser leg, down his sock ... reveals a fresh tattoo.)
　　　　　This is "The Grim Reaper"
　　　　　seventy-five quid
　　　　　three hours twenty-three minutes
　　　　　two needles
　　　　　five colours!
　　　　　it's a traditional design
　　　　　big with bikers
　　　　　you get sickle *and* scythe.
　　　　　brilliant.

　　　　　"The Needlemaster" in Burley.
　　　　　good service.
　　　　　cup of tea if you want
　 and clean
　　　　　spanking clean.

　　　　　not like
(Contempt.)
　　　　　"Body Art Tattooing, Dersingham"!
(Shows a tattoo on his right arm.)
　　　　　Sunburst Dagger of Death.
　　　　　Got done December for Christmas ...
　　　　　needler's a fucking woman ...
　　　　　"Gazza's booked. I'm registered.
　　　　　Take it or leave it ... "
(Suppressed rage.)
　　　　　well, I couldn't come back
　　　　　obviously ...
　　　　　so ...
　　　　　she's jabbing and poking ...
　　　　　one hour forty-three minutes ...
　　　　　came up like a balloon!
　　　　　cunt!
(Tattoo on forearm ...)
　　　　　compared to
　　　　　This.
(Can't remember.)
　　　　　This.

　　　　　Aw. Shit ...

(Strokes tattoo.)
　　　　Madonna and Child
　　　　four colours …
(Herculean struggle to remember …)
　　　　Tattoo Shack!
　　　　The Tattoo Shack!

　　　　Bridgnorth. A456.
　　　　ex-biker
　　　　three hours forty …
　　　　fucking craftsman!
(Other arm, forearm …)
　　　　Chuck's Custom Tattoos.
　　　　I'm not happy with that.
　　　　Too plain.
　　　　I'm going to get it adorned.
(Upper arm …)
　　　　as this.
　　　　I designed that.
　　　　That's an original.
　　　　Angels fighting Devils.
　　　　With Leafy-Tree background.
(Quoting.)
　　　　"Your design or mine.
　　　　Call now or just pop in.
　　　　Thousands of designs to choose from
　　　　professional and friendly." A4112.
　　　　"Sacred Art" … Leominster, this one.

　　　　Good.
(Rubs his newly-tattooed ankle again.)
　　　　Oya.
　　　　Oya.
　　　　Oya.

　　　　I'm going to have to take my mind
　　　　off this
(He stands up, flexing his foot.)
　　　　oh yes
　　　　oh yes
　　　　don't wanna be feeling this all the way back

somebody to talk to
spend a bit of time with
would be ideal
obviously
sun's hot
(Sees something ... becomes very still, focused.)
Hello.
I said "Hello."
Hello.
Hello.
Hello.
(A young girl laughs somewhere ...)

NINE — CHICKENS COMING HOME

Nancy walking ... three or four days later.

NANCY.   sun's so hot.

four days ago
phone call from the police
they think they have some news for us
can they come over?

terrible terrible restlessness anxiety
then two young policemen ... *lads* ...
one with fine soft hair like a kiddie's ...
other lovely polished shoes
pitch up
say ...
"we have apprehended a man in the
unsuccessful attempted abduction of a young girl ...
subsequent inquiries have uncovered a lock-up shed
the earth floor contains the remains of other children
the man is now giving us names
one of them

he says
   is   Rhona"
(Sound of great ice floes breaking up, cracking, churning …)
    I wanted to go out for a walk
    up a hill somewhere

    find some fresh air
    there's no air

Message
after message
after message
on the answerphone
Newspapers
we must we must we must
want to talk to them

Ingrid
comes over
makes something with noodles
can't touch it
but I show willing
twirl it around on the plate a bit with a fork
Ingrid says
"try with chopsticks … I'll show you how to … "
but I leave it all sitting there
dumped on the plate

puts me in mind of worms

I've given Bob some more paracetemol
his headache's approaching Gale Force …

all this time
I've been growing her up
she's been
he's had her buried away …

I wish this weather would break.

I wish it would pour it down.

it's unbearable.

Great Big Storm.
(A huge storm breaks ...)

TEN — SWEATING

Ralph, a cell.

RALPH.
(Hand between his legs.)
        Piss!
        Shit!

        they've just come the questions
        all the time
        all the ... relentless
        without thinking you might need a break
        bit of time to think collect your thoughts ...
        so
        obviously
        when this fucking woman policeman cunt
        comes the nice the interested the ...
        "those are interesting tattoos,
        did you get them all done in the same place?"
        I'm not thinking I'm not sharp enough
        logistically to understand
        that they're putting me in the frame in
        the picture in the *area* for
        the incidents!

        Sunburst Dagger of Death
        logged
        date
        area
        fucking woman needler
        places me in the area where the

dark-haired little …

same
Tattoo Shack, Bridgnorth
kid in the shorts …
I was there
Madonna and Child.

Really, statistically,
once they put that information
with my petrol book and receipts
and the real slip-up in terms of
efficiency over this latest incident …
I've got to let them take me on it!

So I admit
I give them my shed
centre of my operations
they get my special videos

I'm helpful
polite
so
how come then
they're taking turns with the whispering and
    threats …
You're not a man
That's not a man
you're going to have to have ears in your neck boy
in your shoulders in your arse
every second in here
when you eat
think what we've put in there
think about it
and think about bum and knob and what
comes out of there boy … smegma come wank-juice
… I mean, the language …
and even when you're locked up alone don't sleep
boy because all around you we're lying eyes
wide open thinking what next what idea next
for you losing your eye say getting your knob

sliced like a breakfast sausage
somebody shoving somming like this …
up your smelly arse till you shit blood
snot in your food
don't ever rest don't ever sleep
yes, you keep your head down, boy
you keep flicking those eyes about
till we get you!

not on!
oh no
oh no

ELEVEN — NEAR

Nancy, by a window, looking out.

NANCY   police
the fair tufty-haired one said …
there's something you should know …
something he's said …
where he took her …

that shed on Far Forest Lane
He took her there
all the time we were first looking
she was just over there

I went past it!
How many times?

not on her way to my Mother's at all
there
if I'd thought   earlier
got up from *gardening* earlier
gone down there
spotted a light

32

heard a   oh   sound
seen across there
something that made me go across
investigate

she must have known how near I was
if she'd   made a noise
I could have heard her I think
oh

oh
oh
(A sound of clapping ...)

TWELVE — LOVELY TO BE HERE

Agnetha, a large, academic hall somewhere.

AGNETHA. oh
          oh
          oh
          well thank you!
          what a warm reception!
          Thank you!
          I'm very touched. Sincerely.
          It's terrific to be here!
          England. I'm honored.
          London. I'm touched.
          Ladies and Gentlemen ...
          Please. Now ...
          Let me repay you for your very generous Visiting
          Fellowship by ...
          So ...
          Let's see me earn my bucks!
(She gets business-like. Takes up a place behind a lectern. Notes. A screen backs up what she is saying.)
          the title of my thesis is

"Serial Killing ... A Forgivable Act?"
and it is a critical examination of the differences
between crimes of evil
and crimes of illness.
I will base my critique upon
A psychiatric and neurological study of
the criminal brain conducted by myself and colleagues
during my tenure as
Amex-Suntori Chair of Psychiatry
New York University School of Medecine ...

okay
the personal stuff ...
My name is Dr. Agnetha Gottmundsdottir ...
My ancestors came to America
from a small frozen very cold ice-bound
place which experiences for a lot of the time
perpetual night ...
so I guess it is in my Icelandic genes to want to take
myself and you, in my thesis ...
to explore just such a frozen place ...
But I am a *psychiatric* explorer.
So My chosen expedition will be ...
The Arctic frozen sea that is ...
the criminal brain
(Ralph's head lit as if it is an exhibit.)
Let us take a look
*(She walks over to stand behind Ralph, demonstrating around his head,
but not touching. A prison guard stands some way off, watching.)*
The cortex is the thick covering of grey
matter on the upper part of every
human brain
and the function of the cortex
and in particular,
those parts of the cortex
beneath the forehead known as
the frontal lobes
is to modulate the impulses that surge up
from within the brain.
The cortex and the frontal lobes
are there to provide judgement,

to organise behaviour
and decision-making
to learn and stick to
rules of everyday life.
Ladies and Gentlemen ...
they are responsible for making us human.

I intend here to examine
what goes wrong with that humanity ...
which can make certain individuals appear inhuman
using data collected from case studies
conducted by myself and colleagues
of men who have received the death sentence over
the past ten years for their crimes in the US
plus my present case work here in England ...
where of course you have abolished the death penalty.

Ralph Ian Wantage
is currently in Long Larton Maximum Security Prison
serving a life sentence without remission
for the abduction, sexual assault
and murder of seven young girls
over a period of twenty-one years ...

(The light on Ralph extends. Agnetha and Ralph are in the same space.)

RALPH.　　Cunt.

AGNETHA.　Doctor.
　　　　　　Let us be polite with one another, mm?

RALPH.　　I can be polite.
　　　　　　I've got manners.
　　　　　　I'm a gentleman.
　　　　　　Oh yes
　　　　　　Oh yes

AGNETHA.　Yes.
　　　　　　Good.

(Ralph assents ... big accommodating gesture. As she measures his head, he sniffs her. She writes.)

RALPH.　　Cunt.

AGNETHA.　No.
　　　　　　Chanel Number 19
　　　　　　and a mild and gentle soap.
　　　　　　Stop being dangerous, Ralph.

RALPH.   If you know my name,
            you know my reputation.
AGNETHA.   Sure I do.
            Can you hold your hands apart
            like …
            and spread your fingers …
            good …
(He copies her.)
            Interesting tattoo.
RALPH.   Oh no, clever cunt.
            What you after?
AGNETHA.   I'm looking for discontinuous,
            jerky little movements …
(As his fingers, arms jerk …)
            ah-ah.
(She holds up a finger, forty-five degrees to his left.)
            would you let your eyes
            follow my finger, please…?
(His eyes follow jerkily.)
RALPH.   Oh…! Shite.
(She stops.)
AGNETHA.   can we try that again …
            can you try to watch it go smoothly across…?
(Try it again. Jerky again.)
RALPH.   Shite.
AGNETHA.   Okay. Good.
            Now look at the ceiling
            Just with your eyes …
(He cannot.)
RALPH.   Shite.
            This has got to stop!
AGNETHA.   I'm sorry.
            Just …
            please stay still …
(To guard.)
            It's okay …
            I'm just going to …
(She goes behind him, reaches over the top of his head, he starts.)
RALPH.   Hey, no way!
AGNETHA.   … touch him …
            I'm sorry, I did not mean to startle you!

I'm not gonna harm you.
I'm gonna tap you on the nose ...
Just let me ...
(She taps a rhythm on the bridge of his nose. He blinks rapidly, gets distressed as ...)
RALPH.   Hey
                hey
                hey
                hey ...
(Sound of girl laughing ... Lights down on Ralph as Agnetha moves away ... showing us on her own nose.)
AGNETHA. when you tap someone on the
                bridge of the nose, it's reasonable
                for the person to blink a coupla times
                because there is a threat from outside.
                when it's clear there is no threat ...
                a person should be able to accommodate that.
                But if the subject blinks more than three times,
                that's what we call "insufficiency of suppression"
                which may show frontal lobe disfunction.
                The inability to accommodate
                means you can't adapt to a new situation.

                There's a certain rigidity there.

                Like the person is ice-bound

THIRTEEN — SUFFER

Nancy, smoking, her house.

NANCY.   I'd like to see him die
                Watch him
                Suffer
                he wouldn't suffer like she suffered
                but it would be something
                An eye for an eye

tooth for a tooth
I want to see that

everybody at *FLAME*'s
been very understanding
the committee were in absolute agreement
when I suggested we shifted focus
from missing persons …
to spotlight an even more crucial area of
community responsibility …
Paedophile Identification …
Marjorie Alexander pressed my arm
and said "we're with you two hundred percent"
when I get up now
and say

"If we had known
ladies and gentlemen
that within a few hundred yards of us
in a rented lock-up shed
there was a known convicted paedophile …
we would have been vigilant
we would have been forewarned
we would have been able to protect our little girl … "
the clapping is always tumultuous
people always stand up,
a few at first
then it's a full-blown ovation …
we're tapping into something very, very deep here

I got back tonight
somebody from an affiliated organisation's
sent me a video
America
they've got a scheme
you can go and be there when they die
murderers
you get a run-up visit
they show you the electric chair
how it all works
they take you through the procedure

the warders were *very* sympathetic …
the enforcement workers always are …
and then, you can be present,
members of victims' families
at that final moment
he doesn't suffer like she suffered
but it would be something

(A sound of lightning connecting with earth source …)

There was a *grandmother* on the video …
eighty-something, she went …
little grandkiddy shot stone-dead by a killer …
talk about guts!
she goes

(Bad American accent.)

"I kin fergive,
but I kain't fergit."

(English.)

I can forgive,
but I can't forget.
Mother says …
"I'm a forgiving woman
but I can't forgive what he's done.
I'd be there, Nancy, I'd be there … "

Bob says "I'd be there"
I said "If you were there, you'd go for him"
He says "I would … if there were a window of
opportunity, I'd be through it … "
He would.

(Pause.)

All through this, not a peep out of Ingrid.
Eating from a big Economy bag of crisps.
Size of her since she gave up her smoking
and drinking!
Hasn't thought to hand them round.
Just … hugs the bloody bag to herself …
chomping …
suddenly … she says
"I'm going off.
Travelling.
I thought India, Nepal.

The East."

Why?

Why?
Danger
Hot
Filth
Dirt
I don't care.

FOURTEEN — FOUR FARM FUCK

Agnetha, with Ralph, prison. Guard on duty.

AGNETHA. Okay. Good.
give me as many words as you can
that begin with …
F.
RALPH. four
fourteen
forty-four.
(Pause.)
farm.
farm.
farming.
farming.
farm.
farm.
(Pause.)
fuck.
fucker.
fucking.
(He is pleased with these.)
fuck.
AGNETHA. any more, Ralph?
RALPH. four.

                              fourteen.
                              forty-four.
(Pause.)
                              four.
AGNETHA. You've said that, Ralph ...
RALPH.   I'm not fucking stupid!
                              I'm not fucking stupid you know ...
AGNETHA.
(Pats his arm.)
                              Shhh.
                              It's all right.
                              It's not an intelligence test.
                              You do very well in intelligence tests.
                              You're not stupid.
(As she walks away from him.)
                              ... you're manipulative and intense and
                              kinda mesmerising like *a rattlesnake* and you're a
                                    multiple
                              killer and I'd just really like a cigarette suddenly
                              but you're not ...
(Into lecture hall ...)
                              This is not an intelligence test.
                              If I asked Ralph to list ... say ... sixteen products
                              he might buy in a supermarket ...
                              he would do just as well as anyone else ...
RALPH.   beans, lamb chops, pizza, potatoes, Smash,
                              biscuits, lager, whiskey, apples, carrots,
                              crab sticks, steak ... hamburgers ... pop tarts
(Etc. and on ... as ...)
AGNETHA. That is a structured test,
                              with familiar objects.
                              The word-fluency test I have done asks
                              the testee to cope with situations
                              where there are no rules,
                              where they have to improvise,
                              where they make unfamiliar associations.
                              My colleague David Nabkus and I have
                              been conducting these tests for over twenty years ...
(Pause.)
                              sorry.
                              something in my eye.

41

	sorry.
RALPH.	economy sausages
	fish fingers
	frozen peas
AGNETHA.	and

                  Normal is fourteen, give or take ...
                  Anyone who does less than nine ...
                  is abnormal.
                  And falls within mine and David Nabkus' study.

                  We believe Ralph is abnormal
                  and we believe we can show you
                  the reason why ...

                  for what it's worth

                  hey David?

FIFTEEN — ABSOLUTELY NOTHING

Sound of machinery ...

NANCY.	workman plaid shirt

                  came and knocked
                  said
                  "Mrs. Shirley ... we're going to have it down for you
                  that shed
                  do you want to come and watch?"
                  I said
                  "I do"

                  We walked
                  it's no distance
                  and ...
(Nearer machinery ... engines ...)
                  big mechanical digger ...
                  ... big heavy ball ... he climbs in

he says "where shall I start?"
I said
"that front bit where it happened"
and he hit it with the first swing
(A heavy crunch, metal against stone ...)
and the corner of the shed caved in
and he went swinging at it again and again
and
within minutes
it was gone
it was like my heart torn out of my chest
and oh
there was nothing there any more
nothing at all
just nothingness
(A sound of splintering ice floes ...)
oh
help
help
help

Rhona!

Ingrid!

SIXTEEN — THE BRAINS OF IT

AGNETHA. At this stage,
Dr Nabkus, who is the neurologist in our
partnership,
(Slight pause.)
takes a detailed medical history.
In his absence
(Slight pause.)
... I will endeavour to find out
what he would find out ...
(She sits, Ralph circles round her. She watches him for a time.)
You have a little limp there, Ralph ...

RALPH.   No.

AGNETHA. Yes, I think so.

(She watches him as he circles her ... so he stands still, behind her.)

　　　　　Ralph.

　　　　　Don't stand behind me.

RALPH.   It frightens you.

AGNETHA. No.

　　　　　They stop us meeting if you ...

　　　　　Come in front of me.

　　　　　Let me see this limp.

RALPH.   No limp.

(He walks to stand in front of her.)

AGNETHA. Mmmm.

　　　　　Can you hop? On the right leg.

　　　　　For just a little time?

(Rolls his eyes because she is mad ... but hops.)

　　　　　Good.

　　　　　Now the left.

(Ralph does so ... staggers. Far away, something falls from a great height ... fractures ...)

RALPH.　 Shite!

(Tries again.)

　　　　　Shite!

　　　　　Pardon my French.

AGNETHA. Okay.

　　　　　You're just proving something for me.

　　　　　No Big Deal.

　　　　　Come sit down.

　　　　　Talk to me.

(Ralph sits down. Agnetha regards him ... then leans forward and goes to touch his forehead gently. Ralph flinches back, swatting her. She flinches back.)

RALPH.   Sorry!

AGNETHA. Sorry!

RALPH.   Sorry.

AGNETHA. Sorry.

(Both look towards guard. To Guard.)

　　　　　Sorry.

(To Ralph.)

　　　　　I was just going to ask ...

　　　　　how did you get that scar?

RALPH.
(Touches it.)

       This.
       Er.
       I fell off a roof.
       blacked out.
       bosh.
       I was pissed pissed
       and
       I was getting away from somebody
       and
       bosh
       just over and then whack
       nothing broken
       just like this bruise come up fucking large as an egg …

AGNETHA. how old were you?

RALPH.   'bout … eighteen …
       probably … yeah … no no no! … this was a car!
       we got this car … and took it out for a burn yeah …
       and whacked it into a wall yeah …
       I wasn't driving
       obviously
       but I go smack! seat in front …

AGNETHA. this was when you were …

RALPH.   sixteen?
       blood all in my eye

(Right eye.)

       couldn't see fuck when we legged it!
       but
       hey…?
       give us your hand …

AGNETHA.
(To guard.)

       I'm touching him, okay?
       It's just investigative, okay?

(Slowly she does …)

RALPH.   feel there …

AGNETHA. … oh yes …
       what happened there?

RALPH.   I fell down a mine shaft!
       I was blacked out for hours yeah …

                    was running
                    didn't see it just didn't see it ...
                    bosh
                    trip
                    bosh
                    fall
                    whack
                    out!
                    it was serious because it was same place as
                    where my mam threw me in the sink ...
AGNETHA.   when was this?
                    when your mom — mam threw you in the sink?
RALPH.   oh
                    a kid
                    little
                    obviously ...
                    when she could get away with it still!
AGNETHA.   over the years
                    Dr Nabkus and myself have studied
                    more than 250 dangerous criminals ...
                    in significant numbers,
                    these men have incurred physical damage to
                    the brain
                    we have compiled a list of all the
                    verifiable brain injuries suffered by
                    fifteen randomly selected Death Row inmates ...
                    as you will see from the paper ...
                    page five, table D ...
                    the instances are many.

                    After Doctor Nabkus has finished
                    his medical history ...
                    I look for evidence of child abuse ...
(A sound of blustery wind ...)

SEVENTEEN — A LINE OF WASHING

Nancy, her kitchen garden, a pile of washing, a clothes line.
March. Morning.

NANCY.   instead of letters
               telling us where she was
               how she was getting along and whatnot
               these mucky little parcels start arriving
               inside
               cloth squares about this big …
               bright colours
               with foreign-type writing on …
               Handkerchiefs?
               Head Squares?
               Then a postcard …
               "In Lhasa. Hope you got the Tibetan
               prayer flags.
               They are printed with spiritual blessings.
               They are hung up each year
               to signify
                hope
                transformation
               and the spreading of compassion. As the year pro-
                  gresses
               the wind disperses the energy of the words,
               which carry the power to pacify and heal
               everything they touch.
               Lots Of Love.

               Ingrid."

               shoved them in my bits and bobs drawer.
               Daft business.

               Then … the trial starts to happen …
(She starts pegging out …)

I say
can I have our Rhona's remains so we can at least
    bury her ...
letter comes back ...
Ralph Wantage's solicitor insists on keeping the
    remains
as his "exhibits" ...
I carry the letter with me all day ...
it's on the bedside table all night
I don't sleep
I think I am as near to being not alive any more
as I've ever been
I put the letter in my bits and bobs drawer
and there's those flag things

(What she has pegged out are the Tibetan prayer flags. A wind waves them.)

    it's a damn windy day
    they flap and flap and
    the gate opens and
    this thin, thin, brown thing
    says
    "Hello, Mum, it's me.
    See you got the flags then?
    Cool."

    Ingrid.
    Ingrid.
    Ingrid.

EIGHTEEN — CONCLUDING MY ADDRESS

Agnetha, addressing her interested audience. Large, comfortable lecture hall.

AGNETHA. Doctor Nabkus and I
    observed a group of toddlers over three months ...
    half of whom had been subjected to
    serious physical abuse

half of whom had not
We were interested in how the toddlers
responded to a classmate in distress

Here is David's description of "Martin"
an abused boy of thirty-two months ...
(She switches on the tape ... sound of David Nabkus ... we see her listening, watching ...)

    ... he tries to take the hand of the crying
other child, and when she resists, he slaps her
on the arm with his open hand ...
He then turns away from her to look at the ground
and begins vocalising very strongly ...
"cut it out!
CUT IT OUT! ... "
each time saying it a little faster and louder.
He pats her
but she becomes disturbed by his patting ...
so he retreats,
he hisses at her
he bares his teeth ...
then he begins patting her on the back again
his patting becomes beating
and he continues beating her
even though she's screaming ...

(Agnetha is with Ralph in the prison room. Tears are coursing down her cheeks, sobs interrupting her breathing. Ralph is watching her ...)

    Sorry.

RALPH.   Stop.

AGNETHA.   Sorry ... it's just ...

RALPH.   Stop that.

AGNETHA.   I'm sorry.

(A guard, impassive, responds to Agnetha's signs that all is well. Ignores Ralph's agitation ...)

RALPH.   Just stop it
    okay
    okay
    just stop it

AGNETHA.   I'm sorry.
    It's just ... this man ... a good friend of mine ...
    a colleague ...

has died recently …
I'm sorry.
Where were we?

RALPH. You put your chair very close in to the table.
You open your legs as wide as they'll go.
Then I put my hand slowly slowly
down so Chummy over there
sees nothing

AGNETHA. Ralph …
RALPH. and I search with my fingers till they find
your pussy
your knickers are there …
so I go   rip!
my finger ends are touching pussy now.

AGNETHA. Ralph …
I find where you go in.
I position.
Then I ram in
obviously
again and again and again and again
oh yes
oh yes!

AGNETHA. Guard …
you see
the second critical argument in my thesis
is that the mental abuse of children
causes profound and pathological changes in
the structure of the brain as surely as does physical
injury
We brain scanned the children
of severe neglect
We found that entire structures of their cortex
never properly developed …
these cortical regions were twenty to thirty percent
smaller
than normal …

RALPH.
(To Guard.)

What are you looking at?

AGNETHA. abuse also disrupts the brain's stress response system
with profound results …

50

when something traumatic happens …

RALPH.
(To Guard.)

What are you looking at?

AGNETHA. the brain responds by releasing
several waves of hormones …
the last of which is cortisol.

(Somewhere, some liquid starts dripping slowly …)

which is supposed to bring everything back to normal
The problem is … cortisol is toxic …

RALPH. I'm sorry. Sorry.

AGNETHA. if someone is exposed to too much stress
over too long a time …
all that cortisol begins to eat away at the part
of the brain known as the hippocampus
which serves as the brain's archivists …
organising and shaping memories,
putting them in context
placing them in space and time

RALPH. She was asking me something.

AGNETHA. Abuse also affects the relationship between
the left hemisphere of the brain …
which plays a large role in logic and language
and the right hemisphere,
which is thought to play a disproportionately large
role in creativity and expression

RALPH. She was *consulting* with me
obviously
oh yes
oh yes

AGNETHA. in the children we studied
not only was the abnormality twice as high
as a non-abused group,
but in every case
the abnormality was on the left
where *logic* dwells

(A sound of something breaking …)

RALPH. it's a question of the doctor
doing research

AGNETHA. What you get is a kind of erraticness …
they can be very different in one situation

51

	compared to another …
	there is a sense that they don't have a
	larger moral compass …
RALPH.	She likes me!
AGNETHA.	in someone abused or neglected
	the section of the brain involved
	in attachment
	in making emotional bonds
	would actually look different
	the wiring wouldn't be as dense,
	as complex.
RALPH.	she *wants* to spend time with me
AGNETHA.	they are literally lacking some brain organisation
	that allows them to make strong connections
	to other human beings …

(Lights up once again on her and Ralph.)

RALPH.   Was I out of order then?
AGNETHA.   Yeah.
                     Sorta.
                     But it's okay, Ralph.
                     It's not your fault.
                     You can't help it.

NINETEEN — THE BONES OF IT

Nancy, smart outfit, sits on something low, unsuitable, lights cigarette with quivering hand.

NANCY.   Well.
                     Well
                     Well
                     … We've just come from the chapel of rest.
                     They still won't release her bones and …
                     I said "I can't bear it, nothing's moving … "
                     and Ingrid says
                     in her new, quiet, calm … *round* … voice …
                     "let's take some stuff down then …

52

our stuff …
give her some   protection

just been
just now

I thought they'd refuse
red tape
sub judice et cetera
but no …
Mortician showed us straight into the chapel of rest
Her coffin
Ingrid says "We've got some things, we'd like to put
them with her … "
I thought he'd draw the line at that,
but no …
he takes a screwdriver out of his top pocket
unscrews the lid
takes it off and stands with it.
There's two cardboard boxes … different sizes …
DIY-archive system type … we've got them in the
    FLAME
office for files …
Ingrid points to the smaller one …
up the … up the head end …
and says "Is this the skull?"
He nods.
"Go on" she says to me, very quiet, "open it."

it's

it's

it's   beautiful
(Sound of summer garden …)
            I take it out and hold it in my hands
            and
            I can feel her head
            its shape and texture and …
            resilience

and I'm *flooded* with its   *Joy!!!* …
(Bird song, summer insects buzz …)
                    and I say to The Mortician "It's beautiful!"
                    and he just nods
                    because he knows it is
                    well, if anybody would know that he'd know that …
                    and after a while I give it to Ingrid
                    who says "this fantastic brown it is"
                    and she holds it here
(Her heart.)
                    for a long time
                    and then she puts Rhona's witch stone
                    with it back in the box
                    and closes the lid.

                    Bigger box.
                    Ingrid takes the lid off.

                    different parts of her they managed to …
                    I thought top of the arm …
                    collar bone …
                    leg …

                    in there, we put a piece of gorse off
                    her nature table …
                    sheep wool wrapped in it …
                    place she *loved* to go to … windy hill …
                    daft really but …
                    also … Leo The Lion …
                    I go to The Chap … "Guard her, keep her safe"
                    and we all smile.

                    And then … all the lids go back on.
                    He screws the lid back on the coffin
                    and I say
                    Thank you
                    And he says "No problem.
                    I wish more people could be doing this"
(She lights another cigarette. Agitated, angry, unsettled as …)
                    then we come outside into this place.
                    Handy little parky garden place.

I feel at peace.
We're holding hands.
Me and ... *bloody* Ingrid!

and she says ...
"Now Mum ... Be In The Moment"
I say "What, Petal?"
She says "Mum ...
You're in a Very Bad Space.
You've Got To Let Go Of Your Anger.
You've got to Move On.
If You Hold On To Your Rage,
It Will Consume You.
Let It Go.
Make Space for Other Things To Enter Your Heart"
She's got this new way of talking ...
It's like listening to a Diet and Exercise Book.
I said "What do you want me to do?"
 ... (that's how you talk back to them) ...
and she said ...
"I think what we Have To Do
is Forgive Ralph Wantage With Our Whole Hearts"

I said "I want to slap you
I want to spit in your face
I want to scratch you
I want to tear your eyes out with my ... "

She said "She's been dead for twenty years.
It's long enough.
Let Her Go."

I said "I just did, in there"

I couldn't bear to look at her.

She said "You should go and see him.
Tell him you forgive him"

I said "If I go to see him,
I'm taking a gun.

blow his brains all over the wall
I'm taking a knife
slice his thing off
stick the blade through his eye
and take out his brains that thought
what he thought to do what he did …
She was my little girl!"
and she said

(Pause.)

so was I

Forgive that monster
I can't do that
How can I do that?
It's too much

It's too much
It's too much

End of Act One

ACT TWO

TWENTY — A PHONE CALL HOME

Agnetha, drink in one hand, cigarette in the other, circling a telephone. She is thinking about phoning ... sometimes the decision is "no," sometimes it is nearly "yes" ... then, finally, it is, fuck it, "yes" ...

AGNETHA. Hi ...
            Is that ...
            Mary?
            ... you sound like you're in a ... *bathosphere* or something! ...
            do I? ...
            no ... I'm just in *London* ...
(English pronunciation.)
            yeah ...
(Grand.)
            "The *Brit* Lecture"!
            yeah ... the one David and I were gonna ...
            it's ... well ... *kinda weird* ...
            but ... hey ...
            Listen ... how you doing? ...
(She listens.)
            ... well, you would ... you will ...
            ah, Mary ... I know ... I know ...
            but ...
(She listens.)
            Mary ... you just hafta be kind to yourself ...
            and ... give yourself treats ... and ...
            keep warm ...
            and ... make everybody else look after you ...
            Even *The Kids!*
            How are the...?

57

Give 'em a kiss from me, okay?

Hell ... give 'em *Two!*

(She takes a deep breath and ...)

listen, Mary ...

I've did a dumb thing ...

I got drunk and ...

I know I don't ... I don't smoke either ... that's
the *peculiar* thing ...

but okay, I got ... *major pie-eyed* and I ...

sent an E-mail to David

and I'm frightened you got it

oh

you ...

listen ... I'm *really* sor ...

you must have ...

I have to ...

whaddya mean it made you *laugh?* ...

Mary!!!

another woman sends your dead husband a
piece of *Hate* mail and
you *laugh???*

What kinda woman *are* you?

(Beat.)

So it didn't make you ...

You didn't get ...

(Listens really hard ...)

It's just ...

Mary ... I really miss him

I played some footage of him
and ... oh

yeah ... with The Vicious Haircut ...

Mary ... you know I love you ...

(She listens.)

do you ...?

(She shakes her head ...)

thank you ...

that's …
(Agnetha, away from the phone, bends over in agony. Straightens, deep breath, and then …)

I …
no, never mind …
listen …
I'll come see you when I get …
No … I haven't *met* anyone …
apart from serial killers …
This Brit Killer made me an offer I could refuse …
but hey, he's not dating at the present moment …

(Listens.)

… sure he's crazy …

What else is new with me…?

Mary …

Mary …
(She lifts up her hand. The fingers are crossed.)
Oh uh my cab's just pulled up
Gosh it's early
I gotta go …
okay! …
yeah!
right!
You too.
Take Care!
(Phone replaced. Pause. She watches as Nancy walks into a room somewhere.)
Take Care.
(Agnetha, leaving her personal detritus, assuming an authoritative demeanour, walks into the same room as Nancy …)

TWENTY-ONE — TWO CARING WOMEN MEET

NANCY.   I'm "in a very bad space"
I know that.

And I need to "move on"
I know that.
I know I'm ready.
AGNETHA. How?
NANCY.   he
(She has to do this ...)
      took her
she was going to Grandma's for me ...
and he forced her into the van
and
she's ten
and
and he ...
then he wrapped her in polythene sheeting
she was unconscious
but she wasn't dead then
he took her to a *shed* near
and
we *think* he sexually assaulted her
before he held the polythene on her face
and suffocated her
(She is short of breath.)
AGNETHA. *Breathe.*
(Both inhale and exhale, hands on breasts, Nancy sort of following Agnetha ...)
NANCY.   I'm accepting it.
I'm accepting she's dead.
But
(Pause. Somehow an awful admission of guilt ...)
I'm not

and I need to
(The same hand gesture of moving forward ...)
so
he's the   next step

I want to know *why.*
I want to know why *her.*
I want him to know what he's done.
I want him to know how I *feel.*
I want to *understand.*

60

If I could understand *why* ... I might feel ...
it might be ... *better* ... or even just bloody
different ...
I might be able to ...
(For the third time, the hand gesture.)
I've read all the data vis-à-vis the use of
Victim-Offender Communication in the
Treatment of Sexual Abuse and
Violent Crime Trauma ...
My organisation is monitoring all the
Victim-Sensitive Offender Schemes Stateside ...
Research-wise I'm impeccably prepared
I think my letters state that I'm up to
speed.
They said you could help.
Rubber Stamp It.
Fast-Track It.
It's Time.
I want a visit.
(Agnetha stands. Walks to the coffee machine, thinking. Looks back at Nancy.)
AGNETHA. Coffee?
(Nancy shakes her head. Agnetha pours two cups and carries them into the next scene for ...)

TWENTY-TWO — MY CHILDHOOD

Ralph and Agnetha, cup of hot coffee each. Sort of both off duty/role. Guard still there.

RALPH.   ... no ... my *video* collection was in the *back* of the
          shed ... my the *girls* were in the main body of the
          building ...
AGNETHA. but ... *everything* ... wrapped in polythene ... right?
RALPH.   oh yes
          oh yes
AGNETHA. and ... filed?

RALPH.	obviously
	everything was in order
	the whole lay-out made sense
	if they'd *asked* me I'd've taken them through it
	methodically ...
	they needn't have ...
	going in mobhanded ... they destroyed ... the videos ...
	you're looking at about three thousand quid ...
AGNETHA.	... but you see their point, Ralph ...
RALPH.	oh yes still
	coulda been more *organised.*
AGNETHA.	No *remorse* then, Ralphie?
RALPH.	Remorse. So what is that ... remorse?
AGNETHA.	Like Regret. But more.
	It's a feeling of ... *compunction* ...
	of ... deep ... *regret* ...
	you *repent* your sin ...
	last cookie ...
RALPH.	last what?
AGNETHA.	last ...

(Remembers word.)

                ... *biscuit* ... last *biscuit.*
                ... split it?

(Ralph nods. She splits the last biscuit and they share it as.)

                you feel ...
                sorrow
                pity
                compassion ...
                a sort of ... *tender* feeling ...

RALPH.	I can't say I do.

(Pause. Thinks.)

                The only thing I'm sorry about is that
                it's not legal.

AGNETHA.	What's not legal?
RALPH.	Killing girls.

(Agnetha looks at her watch, picks up her writing pad, switches on her tape ... business again.)

AGNETHA.	Tell me about killing girls, Ralph.
RALPH.	No.
	It's Private.

(Pause.)

AGNETHA. Tell me about your childhood then, Ralph.

RALPH. Big kitchen ... we had a big kitchen obviously ...
with filled cupboards ... and shining work surfaces
... and that's where all

the kettles and pans ... copper, all copper, all gleaming

in the light ... because there were lights everywhere ...
spotlights on tracking yeah ... to just touch in a mood
of country ... and a log fire ... with them ... whatsis
... *settles* ...

wood ... pine ... antiquey ... and here is where the
dog sits ...

lies ... when he's not guarding ... or going out on
the hills

with us, *romping* ... and then we come back and
open the

tin of Pal Pedigree dogfood and he gets it, bosh, in
a special new shiny tin on the red stone floor ...

AGNETHA. What kind of dog is he, Ralph?

RALPH. Golden Retriever.
Pedigree. Kennel Club obviously.

AGNETHA. What's his name?

RALPH.

(Pause.)

He doesn't have a name.
We don't go in for names.

(Pause.)

Lassie.

AGNETHA. Tell me about your parents.

RALPH. *Mother* does the meals.
She goes to Safeways and Sainsburys and Tescos
and she gets a *variety* and she doesn't put up with
low standards ...
oh no
oh no
the long pine table *always* has a selection of
... and the *correct* cutlery crockery for different
meals ... and we all sit down to eat together ...

AGNETHA. And what does ... Mother ... cook for you all?

RALPH. Steakmasters ... Oven Cook Chips ... Viennettas ...

After Dinner Mints ... Hamlet Cigars ...

Crusty Warm Bread.

Häagen-Dazs ice cream any many flavours ... Mixed Grills ...

AGNETHA. Is Father there?

RALPH. Yeah. Father. *Dad.*

Except when we're out riding ponies.

Or reading *poytry.*

In the room with all the books on shelves.

And the Nicam Digital television.

AGNETHA. Any Brothers or sisters, Ralph?

RALPH. No.

I'm an only child.

A much-loved only child.

Spoilt rotten.

But what can I do?

AGNETHA.

(She regards him for a time.)

Childhood's kinda private too, huh, Ralph?

RALPH. Yes

oh yes.

(She picks up the biscuit plate. Crumbs on it. Carries it out past the guard.)

AGNETHA. But we know you're a liar, Ralph.

And inconsistent.

We got a few crumbs from you.

(She moistens a forefinger, starts picking up the biscuit crumbs, eating them, as ...)

little bits of you, cookie!

your mom pops you in the sink

step dads arrive

you get chased

you get fucked

up your little bottom, don't you?

up your sad, dirty little ass ...

we're onto you,

you sad, predictable, banal

fuck ...

(She realises she is eating his crumbs. She retches as ...)

"Memo.

Restorative Justice Lobby.

I would not be comfortable in

recommending Mrs. Nancy Shirley
visit Ralph Wantage ... "

TWENTY-THREE — THE SACRED ART OF FENG-SHUI

Nancy, paint-spattered clothes ... a splodge of white paint ludicrously across her face ...

NANCY.   Drip-Free Paint!
           Liars!

           it's big, this room
           with everything out of it.
           spacious.
           you can swing a cat in here now ...

           I'd swing that bloody American Doctor woman
           round by her ...

(Quotes.)

           "the *experiment* is unviable!
           the components *unstable!*"
           Who does she think she *is?*

           I've written some letters
           made some phone calls
           that's what you learn if you run an organisation ...
           Use The Right People!

           I'll get that visit!

           whole house is bigger now ...
           Rhona's kiddie furniture gone
           Bob's stuff ...
           I left a message saying "Will I drop your stuff round?"
           but he's lying low
           Sulking.

Only Ingrid speaks to me.

Nobody else.

They think what I want to do is … criminal …

(Laughs.)

So much for Families

Doesn't matter.

Bob was Yesterday's Newspapers for me anyway.

I said "I'm sorry, but how I felt about you
just hasn't survived …
it didn't keep … like something in the fridge … a
     leftover …
in a jar … and when I picked it up … it was empty
     …
and he said "Don't get *descriptive* with *Me!*
I could have set up with Marie from Nautilus
… why leave it till I'm nearly bloody *Past It?*"
I said "Revenge, Probably" … but I don't mean that.
I don't mean him no harm.
I've got no malice in me.
No nothing.

Just	space
for	
something	fresh
bit of … light	
in the	red

| bit of | fresh air |
| new | feelings |

(It hurts.)

Once this visit's	I might go somewhere
I don't need to be here	
nothing's keeping me	

I'm free to go
(Sound of wings fluttering, not birds … Some beautiful music plays …)

TWENTY-FOUR — CONCLUDING MY ADDRESS

Agnetha at the lectern ... large hall.

AGNETHA. I spoke, in my preamble
of myself as explorer ...
of ... navigating
The Arctic sea of the criminal brain ...
well the expedition is complete
what discoveries do we bring back from that alien
terrain
to help make our own inner and outer landscape
warmer   safer   kinder better?
Cold comfort I'm afraid ...
You see ...
Most forensic psychiatrists tend to buy into the
notion of evil.
I don't.
I can't.
I find no evidence that people are born evil.
To be evil is, dictionary definition, to be "morally
depraved."
To my mind, that bespeaks having conscious control
over something.
The serial murderers I have tested are not in that cat-
egory.
Their deeds themselves are bizarre grotesque
life-destroying
but not evil.
They are driven by forces beyond their control.
The difference between a crime of evil
and a crime of illness is the difference
between a sin and a symptom.
And I guess ... as a moral society ... as a

punishment society …
we can't let the notion of these deeds being "symp-
toms"
intrude in the relationship between
murderers
and the rest of us
because
then we'd have to stop
and observe differently
the distinctions
between right and wrong
between the speakable and unspeakable
between the forgivable and unforgivable
the way sins do …

(Agnetha moves away from the Lectern …)
But when you get back
and you're   cold
you're freezing yourself …
you've got snow in your head …
What then Doctor Gottmundsdottir …
What then Cookie?
don't you cease to be an explorer
and start …
living there?

TWENTY-FIVE — THE VISIT

Prison visiting room. Ralph seated, Nancy at the entrance. A guard.

NANCY.
(To Guard.)
That's him?
(Guard nods … she goes to stand in front of Ralph.)
Ralph Wantage?
(Ralph looks up. Barely nods.)
Nancy Shirley.

You got my letter.

You agreed to see me.

Shall I sit down?

(She does. For a long time, they look, they really look, at one another ...)

RALPH.   She was your kid ...

One of them.

This ...

NANCY.   Rhona.

RALPH.   Rhona.

Funny you coming.

(Pause.)

NANCY.   I want you to know

I forgive you for killing my daughter.

(Silence. Ralph abruptly covers his eye sockets with both hands. Long pause. Guard watches Ralph. Nancy glances at Guard. Ralph brings his hands down, looks somewhere at the corner of her.)

RALPH.

(Very long pause ... then the words sound very rusty ...)

Thank you.

(They sit for a time.)

It's a nice day anyway.

NANCY.   Yes.

There's buds out.

We saw a great *bank* of Pussy willow on the way here.

I should have brought you some.

Are you allowed ... that sort of thing?

(He ignores her. He has no idea if he is allowed that sort of thing. Both glance at Guard. Guard nods. They both look away.)

RALPH.   We can have videos now.

NANCY.   That's nice.

Is that nice?

RALPH.   It's all right.

(Long pause.)

NANCY.   I want you to know

I don't hate you.

RALPH.   Okay.

NANCY.   I used to.

But I don't any more.

RALPH.   Okay.

NANCY.   My daughter ... Ingrid ... said ... Let It Go ...

Like A Bird Into The Wind.

	She's Spiritual.
RALPH.	How old is she?
NANCY.	thirty-three
RALPH.	Oh.

(He is not interested.)

NANCY.	I've brought some photographs.
	Would you like to see them?
RALPH.	Of ... her?
NANCY.	Rhona.
	And our family. Ingrid. Bob. My husband.

(She gets them out. A small dog-eared selection.)

NANCY.	That's Rhona as a baby.

(Hands them to him in turn ...)

That's me holding her.

This is Ingrid, that's her sister, holding her.

This is them holding their pets.

Her cat is Fluff

Ingrid's holding Black-and-White.

You can see why they're called that ... because she's fluffy ... and he's ... see...?

This is Rhona with Ingrid and my husband Bob.

We were on a day out.

I took it ... it's uneven ground ...

that's why they're slightly ...

(Her body indicates leaning ...)

This is Rhona dressed as an octopus.

For a fancy-dress competition.

RALPH.	Did she win?
NANCY.	She came third.
	Behind Little Miss Muffet
	and a Loch Ness Monster.

(She points them out.)

RALPH.	She should have won.
NANCY.	That's what we thought.
	But we were biased obviously.
RALPH.	That's good those arms.
	How did you do them?
NANCY.	She did them.
	Rhona.
	They're wire she made into springs.
	When you touched them,

70

they ...

(Body language shivers and vibrates ...)

RALPH.   I don't think I hurt her.

NANCY.   You did.

RALPH.   I don't think she was frightened at all ...

NANCY.   She must have been.

(Ralph thinks for a long time. Nancy watches him carefully. When he looks up suddenly, she holds his gaze. He looks away ... she touches his arm ...)

RALPH.   You're not allowed to touch.

NANCY.   Sorry.

(Guard is watching. She removes her hand. Both sit back.)

NANCY.   But she must have been frightened!

(Ralph keeps thinking ...)

RALPH.   Do you live on a farm
            and ride horses
            and read poytry
            and have warm bread?

NANCY.   Not on a farm
            No horses
            We aren't particular big on poetry.
            Books though.
            Yes. Sometimes. Warm bread.
            On cold days. You just pop it in the oven on
            a low heat. Few minutes ...

(Ralph nods. He knew this.)

            Did your mother ever...?

RALPH.   Oh yes
            Oh yes

(She didn't.)

NANCY.   And your dad? What did he do?

RALPH.   my dad
            well
            he was the disciplinarian
            obviously

NANCY.   Made you behave, did he?

RALPH.   oh yes
            oh yes
            say you swore filthy language
            he's got you by the hair here

(Back of neck.)

71

and you're in the washing up water
bosh, wash your mouth out with soap water!
or you done wrong
anything!
he's
(In Dad's voice.)
See it in my eyes, twat?
Can you see it, you fucking little pillock?
I'm looking into you and I'm seeing shit!
You keep yourself clean!
You hear me?
(Sound of a thump on flesh … Ralph registers it, side of head.)
You deaf little bugger!
(Another thump, same side of head. Ralph's body registers it.)
You listening to me?
Your head
(Tap on forehead.)
taking this in?
I'll make sure you hear what I say …
Stand still
Stand still
Stand still
you stand still and don't move one muscle
not one
you don't even blink, twat
until I know you know I mean what I say.
"See it in my eyes, twat?"
(Ralph is blinking rapidly.)
NANCY.   Frightening bugger.
(Ralph nods.)
Hurt you a lot.
(Ralph, after a time, nods.)
Can you see it hurt Rhona then?
Can you see it frightened her?
What you did.
(Ralph thinks impassive for a long time. Then …)
RALPH.   Yes.
(He nods.)
(Nods more times.)
(Tears in his eyes.)
(He wipes them fiercely. Violently.)

(Dry painful sobs start.)
(Awful, embarassing, rusty crying.)
(Nancy watches. Guard watches. He holds his chest in pain as he sub-sides. Calmly, she takes out a tissue. Holds it up to Guard questioningly. He nods slightly, dismissively. Nancy hands it to Ralph. He uses it. Puts it on the table between them. Guard watches.)

      Don't come and bother me again.

      Cunt.

(A pause. Then, a genuine apology ...)

      Pardon my French.

(Nancy exits. Guard stands over Ralph. Ralph stands, then walks in a circle round his cell.)

TWENTY-SIX — LETTER-WRITING

Ralph, communal area, writing ... interruptive loud music playing off centre ...

RALPH.   Dear Mrs. Shirley ...
                Dear Nancy ...
                Dear Mrs. Shirley ...
                I am writing to you ...
                I am sorry ...
                I am *very* sorry ...
                I am sorry ...
                I am sorry that I murdered ...
                I am sorry that I abused ...
                I am sorry that I ...

                turn the *fucking* music!!!
                turn the *fucking* noise down!!!
                You ... Fuck! ... down!!!

                Down!

                Bit of fucking *peace* ... Jesus!
(He aligns his stationery and pens into neatness. And again. And again.)

I am sorry.
I am sorry from the bottom of my heart.

I am thinking about what I did.

I am thinking about what I did

I am realising

I realise in abusing and killing your daughter

... *Rhona* ...

I   hurt   her

you
(He realigns the paper ... pen ... envelope. And again.)
Oh Christ.
(He spits on the paper, folds it carefully, puts it in the envelope. Seals it. Tears it up. He starts to collect and align the torn pieces into a pile as ...)

Fucking Music!

TWENTY-SEVEN — SOMETHING AWFUL

Nancy, a cup of morning tea, a dressing gown ... a sachet of resolve.

NANCY.   Well!
Well!
Well ... I'll go to sea on a duck's back!
Nancy Shirley!
Nancy Shirley how could you?
I've just done something *awful!*
I've been out on a *DATE!*
With a *Man!*
Roy Taylor!
Roy Taylor!

To a *Chinese Restaurant!*
Mince in *lettuce* leaves you eat with your fingers
and Prawns in ginger and ...
all this *washed down* with some sort of
Oriental wine
and I get tiddly and
you know what's coming next
he says "can I come in for a bit"
and I say "Lovely"
and next thing we're up there
doing ... well ... you can imagine!

Ingrid dropped by with this ...
... "Remorse" ...

(Looks closer.)

... "Resolve" ... Resolve ...

Ingrid says she understands

Which is more than I do!

She says "It's The Life Force"

The Wine Talking More Like!

I said "This isn't *Me* ... Ingrid ... "

She said "He's not bad looking ... "

I said "*Please* don't tell your father!"

Life Force!

She talks such ... *hocus pocus!*

TWENTY-EIGHT — QUIET AND SILENCE

Agnetha and Ralph, prison room ... a tape recorder ... notes.
Agnetha closes her notebook.

AGNETHA. Well, Ralph. This is my last visit.
I wondered if you wanted to tell me anything more.
And I came to say "Goodbye"

RALPH. Can you turn that thing off?
(Tape.)
I've been wanting to tell you things I
don't want recorded, yeah?

AGNETHA. Okay.
(Turns off the tape.)
Yes?

RALPH. I think I've caught something.
I think I caught cancer or something.
Here.
That's lungs right?
Lung cancer.
And that's me not even fucking smoking!

AGNETHA. What does the doctor say?

RALPH. Says it's just Stress!
Fucking Shite!
Fucking Quack cunt!
Stress is in here
(Forehead.)
I know where
Fucking Stress Is!
This fucking *gnawing*, Here!
(Chest.)
Not Fucking Stress!

AGNETHA. Where is this pain, Ralph?
(He shows her ...)
That's your heart, Ralph.
Did the doctor check out your heart?

RALPH. Says there's nothing fucking *wrong*

with the heart!

Fucking Quack Cunt!

AGNETHA. How long have you been in pain, Ralph?

RALPH. Er ...

It started ... night after that mother of that
girl Rhona I done came ... that was Thursday ...
so ...

(Counts on his fingers.)

It's been a bit.

AGNETHA. Mrs. Shirley came to see you?

I recommended she ...

RALPH. Yes, well ... you were overruled by
The Doctor-in-Charge of Nutting-Off
weren't you?

AGNETHA. And she visited with you?

RALPH. Yes.

She's forgive me, actually.

We're straight on it.

(Spasm in his chest.)

Oya

Oya

Oya.

AGNETHA. I think you should talk to your doctor again.

Ask to see a psychologist.

What you are feeling may be psychological.

What you are feeling may be

Remorse.

And that will be very painful for you

Ralph.

Try rub it ... here.

(She shows him on herself ... middle of the chest, just below the sternum.)

RALPH. Fucking hurts.

Burns.

Eats.

Gnaws.

Fucking Cancer.

AGNETHA. Well. I'm sorry.

I hope they find out what it is and ...

sort it out.

So.

This is Goodbye.

(She stands.)
                    Take care.
                    Bye Ralph.
(To Guard.)
                    Sue me.
(Ralph tidies and realigns everything on the table top. And again. And again …)
RALPH.   It's a question of finding a window
                    of opportunity
                    of always being ready
                    of always doing research
                    of committing yourself to
                    the rehearsal
                    the training
                    for practising
                    for when that
                    one golden moment
                    shines
                    Oh yes
                    Oh yes
(Beautiful, haunting music plays.)

TWENTY-NINE — HOW HE DOES IT, WHY HE DOES IT

Ralph, in his cell, sweating, training gear. Working out …

RALPH.   It's all a question of energy expended
                    vee calorie intake, yeah?
                    Fitness is what it's all about
                    Which is twenty-percent genetic
                    and eighty-percent working at it yourself
                    You can beat any condition if
                    you got a healthy body
                    oh yes
                    oh yes
                    fifteen

sixteen
seventeen eighteen
nineteen
twenty
yes!!!

(He drops. Unwinds a long cloth from round his neck. Wipes the sweat from his brow, body. One of his tattoos catches his eye. Looks at it carefully, fondly.)

Angels Fighting Devils.

(Goes to a chair. Sits in it.)

Fucking craftsman.

(He stands up, slings the cloth over the pull-up bar. With his belt he fashions a noose. Stands on his chair.)

Gnawed to death?

I don't think so.

(He completes his preparations. Kicks the chair away from him. He hangs, choking, jerking as ...)

Hello

Hello

Hello

Hell

He ...

(A burst of wild, beautiful music plays ...)

THIRTY — GRAVESIDE

Nancy, in a Memorial Garden. Some church-like music off to the side comes to an end. Agnetha, entering, watches her for a few seconds.

AGNETHA. Not a *big* funeral ...

NANCY. Bit of a surprise ... person with his talent for putting sunshine in everybody's life ...

AGNETHA. I think the old lady in the black fur was his mother ...

NANCY. His foster mother.

AGNETHA. She looked ... bad ...

NANCY. Not as bad as if she had been his mother ...

(Agnetha thinks about this …)

AGNETHA. Yes. Yes.

I think that would be unbearable.

NANCY. Actually, nothing's unbearable.

AGNETHA. You went to see him.

NANCY. And you tried to stop me.

AGNETHA. I was trying to protect everybody.

NANCY. Him.

AGNETHA. Everybody.

NANCY. Him.

How much time and energy did you give him?

And me?

And the others?

Cigarette?

AGNETHA.

(Wants to, but …)

I'm trying not to …

NANCY. me too.

(Puts hers away too.)

You look upset.

Were you fond of Ralph?

AGNETHA. It's not for Ralph …

It's for somebody else.

For me.

NANCY. Me as well.

I couldn't feel much for him really …

AGNETHA. No.

It was …

not easy.

(Both nod thoughtfully.)

NANCY. Do you think he did it …

the … suicide …

Ralph …

because I went to see him…?

(Long silence.)

AGNETHA. yes.

(Long silence.)

NANCY. I don't know whether to be sad or glad.

AGNETHA. be both.

NANCY. No.

Bugger it.

I've been sad enough.
I'll be glad.
That murdering bugger's kept me from
happiness
and ... laughing
and
cheer
for bloody twenty-odd years ...
Bugger it.
Glad.
Laugh.
Have a joke.

AGNETHA. My colleague and best friend,
David ...
told jokes ...

NANCY. Does he?

AGNETHA. Did. Told. He died three months ago ...
stupid accident ...
wearing a seat belt ...
observing the speed limit ...
a truck goes out of control ...
the driver is on crack ...
the truck smashes the car ...
the truck driver is unhurt.
David ...

(Nancy takes Agnetha's hand. Very matter of fact.)
Anyhow.
Good joke from him.
These two lovers decide to commit suicide.
They both work in the same office.
So they put arsenic in their sandwiches ...
go to work
twelve-thirty
they eat them.
It's a Suicide Pact Lunch.

(Both women smile ... laugh? ...)
NANCY.
(Acknowledges.)
Suicide Pact Lunch.

AGNETHA. I worked with him every day for ten years.
Two days before he died ...

I slept with him.

It just happened.

His wife is a very good friend.

Why am I telling you this?
NANCY.   Why are you?
AGNETHA. Do I tell her?
NANCY.   No.
You just suffer.

"the difference between a crime of evil
and a crime of illness is the difference
between a sin and a symptom ... "

Your words.

I read your thesis ...
You knew what you were doing.
Live with it.
(Near, the sound of doleful funereal music from the crematorium chapel.)
Oh, perfect.
another funeral...!
(The sun breaks through, birds twitter, music plays, Nancy smiles at Agnetha as ...)

End of Play

PROPERTY LIST

Airline tickets (AGNETHA)
Passport (AGNETHA)
Carry-on bag (AGNETHA)
Towel (RALPH)
Hand lotion (RALPH)
Stuffed toy lion (NANCY)
Stone with hole in it (NANCY)
Suitcase (RALPH, AGNETHA)
Videos (RALPH)
Notebook (RALPH, AGNETHA)
Paper and writing utensil (RALPH)
Laptop (AGNETHA)
Plastic cup (AGNETHA)
Small bottles of brandy (AGNETHA)
Drink (NANCY, AGNETHA)
Notes (AGNETHA)
Cigarette (NANCY, AGNETHA)
Pile of washing (NANCY)
Clothespins (NANCY)
Tibetan prayer flags (NANCY)
Lighter or matches (NANCY)
Telephone (AGNETHA)
Pot of coffee (AGNETHA)
Cups (AGNETHA, NANCY)
Cookie on plate (AGNETHA)
Writing pad (AGNETHA)
Tape recorder (AGNETHA)
Photos (NANCY)
Tissue (NANCY)
Paperwork (AGNETHA)
Clothing (AGNETHA)
Envelope (RALPH)
Sachet (NANCY)
Long cloth (RALPH)

SOUND EFFECTS

New York street sounds
Large plane flying
Buzz of an English garden
Van accelerating
Snipping of plants
Wind
Romantic music
Sounds of summer countryside
Car driving off
Ping of in-flight "fasten seat belts" sign
Sounds of time markers: New Year's bells, bonfire fireworks,
    Christmas, clocks
Young girl laughing
Ice floes breaking up
Huge storm
Clapping
Lightning connecting with earth source
Busy street market/bazaar: foreign voices, business
Machinery
Something falling from a great height
Male voice speaking
Liquid dripping
Something breaking
Sound of summer garden: bird song, insects
Wings fluttering
Beautiful music
Sound of person being hit
Loud music
Phone ringing
Church-like music
Funereal music
Birds twittering

NEW PLAYS

★ **YELLOW FACE by David Henry Hwang.** Asian-American playwright DHH leads a protest against the casting of Jonathan Pryce as the Eurasian pimp in the original Broadway production of *Miss Saigon*, condemning the practice as "yellowface." The lines between truth and fiction blur with hilarious and moving results in this unreliable memoir. "A pungent play of ideas with a big heart." —*Variety.* "Fabulously inventive." —*The New Yorker.* [5M, 2W] ISBN: 978-0-8222-2301-6

★ **33 VARIATIONS by Moisés Kaufmann.** A mother coming to terms with her daughter. A composer coming to terms with his genius. And, even though they're separated by 200 years, these two people share an obsession that might, even just for a moment, make time stand still. "A compellingly original and thoroughly watchable play for today." —*Talkin' Broadway.* [4M, 4W] ISBN: 978-0-8222-2392-4

★ **BOOM by Peter Sinn Nachtrieb.** A grad student's online personal ad lures a mysterious journalism student to his subterranean research lab. But when a major catastrophic event strikes the planet, their date takes on evolutionary significance and the fate of humanity hangs in the balance. "Darkly funny dialogue." —*NY Times.* "Literate, coarse, thoughtful, sweet, scabrously inappropriate." —*Washington City Paper.* [1M, 2W] ISBN: 978-0-8222-2370-2

★ **LOVE, LOSS AND WHAT I WORE by Nora Ephron and Delia Ephron, based on the book by Ilene Beckerman.** A play of monologues and ensemble pieces about women, clothes and memory covering all the important subjects—mothers, prom dresses, mothers, buying bras, mothers, hating purses and why we only wear black. "Funny, compelling." —*NY Times.* "So funny and so powerful." —*WowOwow.com.* [5W] ISBN: 978-0-8222-2355-9

★ **CIRCLE MIRROR TRANSFORMATION by Annie Baker.** When four lost New Englanders enrolled in Marty's community center drama class experiment with harmless games, hearts are quietly torn apart, and tiny wars of epic proportions are waged and won. "Absorbing, unblinking and sharply funny." —*NY Times.* [2M, 3W] ISBN: 978-0-8222-2445-7

★ **BROKE-OLOGY by Nathan Louis Jackson.** The King family has weathered the hardships of life and survived with their love for each other intact. But when two brothers are called home to take care of their father, they find themselves strangely at odds. "Engaging dialogue." —*TheaterMania.com.* "Assured, bighearted." —*Time Out.* [3M, 1W] ISBN: 978-0-8222-2428-0

DRAMATISTS PLAY SERVICE, INC.
440 Park Avenue South, New York, NY 10016 212-683-8960 Fax 212-213-1539
postmaster@dramatists.com www.dramatists.com

NEW PLAYS

★ **A CIVIL WAR CHRISTMAS: AN AMERICAN MUSICAL CELEBRA-TION by Paula Vogel, music by Daryl Waters.** It's 1864, and Washington, D.C. is settling down to the coldest Christmas Eve in years. Intertwining many lives, this musical shows us that the gladness of one's heart is the best gift of all. "Boldly inventive theater, warm and affecting." *–Talkin' Broadway.* "Crisp strokes of dialogue." *–NY Times.* [12M, 5W] ISBN: 978-0-8222-2361-0

★ **SPEECH & DEBATE by Stephen Karam.** Three teenage misfits in Salem, Oregon discover they are linked by a sex scandal that's rocked their town. "Savvy comedy." *–Variety.* "Hilarious, cliché-free, and immensely entertaining." *–NY Times.* "A strong, rangy play." *–NY Newsday.* [2M, 2W] ISBN: 978-0-8222-2286-6

★ **DIVIDING THE ESTATE by Horton Foote.** Matriarch Stella Gordon is determined not to divide her 100-year-old Texas estate, despite her family's declining wealth and the looming financial crisis. But her three children have another plan. "Goes for laughs and succeeds." *–NY Daily News.* "The theatrical equivalent of a page-turner." *–Bloomberg.com.* [4M, 9W] ISBN: 978-0-8222-2398-6

★ **WHY TORTURE IS WRONG, AND THE PEOPLE WHO LOVE THEM by Christopher Durang.** Christopher Durang turns political humor upside down with this raucous and provocative satire about America's growing homeland "insecurity." "A smashing new play." *–NY Observer.* "You may laugh yourself silly." *–Bloomberg News.* [4M, 3W] ISBN: 978-0-8222-2401-3

★ **FIFTY WORDS by Michael Weller.** While their nine-year-old son is away for the night on his first sleepover, Adam and Jan have an evening alone together, beginning a suspenseful nightlong roller-coaster ride of revelation, rancor, passion and humor. "Mr. Weller is a bold and productive dramatist." *–NY Times.* [1M, 1W] ISBN: 978-0-8222-2348-1

★ **BECKY'S NEW CAR by Steven Dietz.** Becky Foster is caught in middle age, middle management and in a middling marriage—with no prospects for change on the horizon. Then one night a socially inept and grief-struck millionaire stumbles into the car dealership where Becky works. "Gently and consistently funny." *–Variety.* "Perfect blend of hilarious comedy and substantial weight." *–Broadway Hour.* [4M, 3W] ISBN: 978-0-8222-2393-1

DRAMATISTS PLAY SERVICE, INC.
440 Park Avenue South, New York, NY 10016 212-683-8960 Fax 212-213-1539
postmaster@dramatists.com   www.dramatists.com

NEW PLAYS

★ **AT HOME AT THE ZOO by Edward Albee.** Edward Albee delves deeper into his play THE ZOO STORY by adding a first act, HOMELIFE, which precedes Peter's fateful meeting with Jerry on a park bench in Central Park. "An essential and heartening experience." –*NY Times.* "Darkly comic and thrilling." –*Time Out.* "Genuinely fascinating." –*Journal News.* [2M, 1W] ISBN: 978-0-8222-2317-7

★ **PASSING STRANGE book and lyrics by Stew, music by Stew and Heidi Rodewald, created in collaboration with Annie Dorsen.** A daring musical about a young bohemian that takes you from black middle-class America to Amsterdam, Berlin and beyond on a journey towards personal and artistic authenticity. "Fresh, exuberant, bracingly inventive, bitingly funny, and full of heart." –*NY Times.* "The freshest musical in town!" –*Wall Street Journal.* "Excellent songs and a vulnerable heart." –*Variety.* [4M, 3W] ISBN: 978-0-8222-2400-6

★ **REASONS TO BE PRETTY by Neil LaBute.** Greg really, truly adores his girlfriend, Steph. Unfortunately, he also thinks she has a few physical imperfections, and when he mentions them, all hell breaks loose. "Tight, tense and emotionally true." –*Time Magazine.* "Lively and compulsively watchable." –*The Record.* [2M, 2W] ISBN: 978-0-8222-2394-8

★ **OPUS by Michael Hollinger.** With only a few days to rehearse a grueling Beethoven masterpiece, a world-class string quartet struggles to prepare their highest-profile performance ever—a televised ceremony at the White House. "Intimate, intense and profoundly moving." –*Time Out.* "Worthy of scores of bravissimos." –*BroadwayWorld.com.* [4M, 1W] ISBN: 978-0-8222-2363-4

★ **BECKY SHAW by Gina Gionfriddo.** When an evening calculated to bring happiness takes a dark turn, crisis and comedy ensue in this wickedly funny play that asks what we owe the people we love and the strangers who land on our doorstep. "As engrossing as it is ferociously funny." –*NY Times.* "Gionfriddo is some kind of genius." –*Variety.* [2M, 3W] ISBN: 978-0-8222-2402-0

★ **KICKING A DEAD HORSE by Sam Shepard.** Hobart Struther's horse has just dropped dead. In an eighty-minute monologue, he discusses what path brought him here in the first place, the fate of his marriage, his career, politics and eventually the nature of the universe. "Deeply instinctual and intuitive." –*NY Times.* "The brilliance is in the infinite reverberations Shepard extracts from his simple metaphor." –*TheaterMania.* [1M, 1W] ISBN: 978-0-8222-2336-8

DRAMATISTS PLAY SERVICE, INC.
440 Park Avenue South, New York, NY 10016 212-683-8960 Fax 212-213-1539
postmaster@dramatists.com   www.dramatists.com

NEW PLAYS

★ **AUGUST: OSAGE COUNTY by Tracy Letts.** WINNER OF THE 2008 PULITZER PRIZE AND TONY AWARD. When the large Weston family reunites after Dad disappears, their Oklahoma homestead explodes in a maelstrom of repressed truths and unsettling secrets. "Fiercely funny and bitingly sad." –*NY Times*. "Ferociously entertaining." –*Variety.* "A hugely ambitious, highly combustible saga." –*NY Daily News*. [6M, 7W] ISBN: 978-0-8222-2300-9

★ **RUINED by Lynn Nottage.** WINNER OF THE 2009 PULITZER PRIZE. Set in a small mining town in Democratic Republic of Congo, RUINED is a haunting, probing work about the resilience of the human spirit during times of war. "A full-immersion drama of shocking complexity and moral ambiguity." –*Variety.* "Sincere, passionate, courageous." –*Chicago Tribune.* [8M, 4W] ISBN: 978-0-8222-2390-0

★ **GOD OF CARNAGE by Yasmina Reza, translated by Christopher Hampton.** WINNER OF THE 2009 TONY AWARD. A playground altercation between boys brings together their Brooklyn parents, leaving the couples in tatters as the rum flows and tensions explode. "Satisfyingly primitive entertainment." –*NY Times*. "Elegant, acerbic, entertainingly fueled on pure bile." –*Variety.* [2M, 2W] ISBN: 978-0-8222-2399-3

★ **THE SEAFARER by Conor McPherson.** Sharky has returned to Dublin to look after his irascible, aging brother. Old drinking buddies Ivan and Nicky are holed up at the house too, hoping to play some cards. But with the arrival of a stranger from the distant past, the stakes are raised ever higher. "Dark and enthralling Christmas fable." –*NY Times*. "A timeless classic." –*Hollywood Reporter.* [5M] ISBN: 978-0-8222-2284-2

★ **THE NEW CENTURY by Paul Rudnick.** When the playwright is Paul Rudnick, expectations are geared for a play both hilarious and smart, and this provocative and outrageous comedy is no exception. "The one-liners fly like rockets." –*NY Times*. "The funniest playwright around." –*Journal News*. [2M, 3W] ISBN: 978-0-8222-2315-3

★ **SHIPWRECKED! AN ENTERTAINMENT—THE AMAZING ADVENTURES OF LOUIS DE ROUGEMONT (AS TOLD BY HIMSELF) by Donald Margulies.** The amazing story of bravery, survival and celebrity that left nineteenth-century England spellbound. Dare to be whisked away. "A deft, literate narrative." –*LA Times*. "Springs to life like a theatrical pop-up book." –*NY Times*. [2M, 1W] ISBN: 978-0-8222-2341-2

DRAMATISTS PLAY SERVICE, INC.
440 Park Avenue South, New York, NY 10016 212-683-8960 Fax 212-213-1539
postmaster@dramatists.com   www.dramatists.com